Going to Work ANIMAL EDITION · Going to Work ANIMAL EDITION · Going to Work ANIMAL EDITION · Going to Wo
ANIMAL EDITION · Going to Work ANIMAL EDITION · Going to Work ANIMAL EDITION · Going to Work ANIMAL EDITI
Going to Work ANIMAL EDITION · Going to Work ANIMAL EDITION · Going to Work ANIMAL EDITION · Going to Wo
ANIMAL EDITION · Going to Work ANIMAL EDITION · Going to Work ANIMAL EDITION · Going to Wo

Going To Work
ANIMAL EDITION

Military
Animals

ABDO
Publishing Company

A Buddy **Book by**
Julie Murray

VISIT US AT

www.abdopublishing.com

Published by ABDO Publishing Company, 8000 West 78th Street, Edina, Minnesota 55439.

Copyright © 2009 by Abdo Consulting Group, Inc. International copyrights reserved in all countries. No part of this book may be reproduced in any form without written permission from the publisher. Buddy Books™ is a trademark and logo of ABDO Publishing Company.

Printed in the United States.

Coordinating Series Editor: Rochelle Baltzer
Editor: Sarah Tieck
Contributing Editor: Marcia Zappa
Graphic Design: Maria Hosley
Cover Photograph: *U.S. Navy:* Mr. John F. Williams
Interior Photographs/Illustrations: *Clipart.com* (pp. 10, 11, 15, 30); *iStockPhoto:* Hulton Archive (p. 9); Spc. Cheryl Ransford, USA (p. 15); *U.S. Air Force:* Senior Airman Domonique Simmons (p. 5), Airman Chad Warren (p. 14); *U.S. Army:* John Byerly, Civ. (p. 25), Christine June (p. 17), Petty Officer 1st Class Sean Mulligan (p. 19), Michelle Owens (p. 13); *U.S. Marine Corps:* Pfc. Shawn M. Statz (p. 26); *U.S. Navy:* Mass Communications Specialist Seaman Daisy Abonza (p. 21), Photographers Mate 1st Class Brien Aho (p. 23), Petty Officer 2nd Class Katrina Beeler (p. 29), Photographers Mate 3rd Class Jamar X. Perry (p. 7), Mass Communications Specialist 2nd Class Jennifer A. Villalovos (pp. 13, 22), Mr. John F. Williams (p. 7).

Library of Congress Cataloging-in-Publication Data

Murray, Julie, 1969-
  Military animals / Julie Murray.
    p. cm. -- (Going to work--animal edition)
  ISBN 978-1-60453-562-4
  1. Animals--War use--Juvenile literature. I. Title.

UH87.M87 2009
355.4'24--dc22
                                                              2008043604

Contents

Animals At Work

Going to work is an important part of life. At work, people use their skills to accomplish tasks and earn money.

Animals can have jobs, too. Many times, they complete tasks that human workers can't.

Some animals work in the military. They save lives and help guard nations. This is worthwhile work.

Animals are important members of the armed forces. Many nations, including the United States, use military animals.

Helping Out

Military animals are specially trained workers. They may aid soldiers. Some even go into battle during war!

Animals do a variety of jobs to keep people safe. Dogs find **bombs** and enemies. And, sea animals serve by doing jobs deep underwater.

Militaries use animals for jobs that humans, machines, and computers cannot do.

HISTORY LESSON

Military animals have been important helpers since ancient times. Before **tanks** and motor vehicles were invented, soldiers rode horses into battle.

Sometimes, people traveled on camels or elephants. Other times, large animals helped move objects. Mules and oxen could carry heavy loads, too.

In India, elephants were used in war earlier than 400 BC!

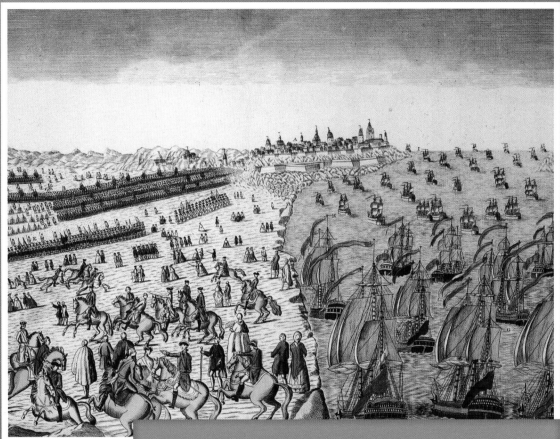

Starting in 1775, Americans fought for freedom from Great Britain in the American Revolution. Americans used horses to help them win battles. They won the war in 1783.

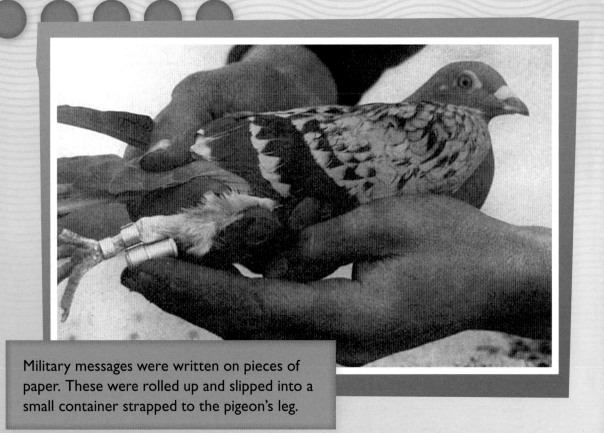

Military messages were written on pieces of paper. These were rolled up and slipped into a small container strapped to the pigeon's leg.

Before radios, soldiers sent messages with carrier pigeons. The birds were trained to fly to a location. Pigeons are naturally skilled at finding their home base.

Carrier pigeons were very important to soldiers. During World War I, a pigeon named Cher Ami received an award. Cher Ami delivered a message after being shot. This saved 200 soldiers!

As early as **World War I (1914-1918)**, some military pigeons were fitted with tiny cameras. They would fly over the enemy and take spy pictures.

Did You Know?

Working Together

Military animals are not pets. They aid land, air, and sea forces. Each animal receives special training. It is based on the animal and the work to be done.

In general, trainers teach animals to follow commands and do simple tasks. This can take weeks, months, or even years!

During training, animals do practice drills.

Sometimes when military dogs retire, they are adopted by families.

13

Many military animals are comfortable riding in planes and helicopters. It is part of their job!

Military animals travel throughout the world to do special jobs. They fly in planes and ride on boats to reach new lands.

Many military animals travel to places where people are fighting. To stay safe, they may wear protective gear.

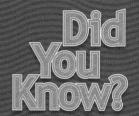

Many years ago. military animals had armor and shields like soldiers. Today. they wear gear such as gas masks and bulletproof vests.

Serve And Protect

Dogs are well suited for military work. In the dark, they see better than humans. And, they can smell and hear very well. In fact, a dog's sense of smell is more than 50 times stronger than a human's! These natural abilities are put to good use in the military.

A military dog mainly works with one person, or handler. The dog and its handler form a team. The dog protects its handler. It is trained to attack only when commanded.

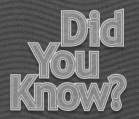
Sometimes, military dogs sense things human soldiers do not. This helps them protect soldiers and surprise enemies before attacking.

Dogs work with air, land, and sea forces. They help with patrolling and law **enforcement**. This is called sentry work.

They also **scout** for hidden enemies. This helps protect soldiers and bases from surprise attacks.

Military dogs are able to sniff out bombs before they explode.

Under The Sea

Sea animals, such as sea lions and dolphins, are also military helpers. Sea lions are smart, curious creatures. They have excellent hearing and can see in dark waters.

Sea lions use their natural skills to guard military ships. They are trained to find unknown swimmers. If they find one, they **clamp** the swimmer's legs. This traps the swimmer until the military learns his or her purpose.

20

Sea lions are part of the U.S. Navy Marine Mammal Program.

21

Dolphins can stay deep underwater for a long time. There, they can complete tasks that humans cannot.

Dolphins are also well suited to being military animals. They have a special sense called **echolocation**. This helps them find things underwater.

The U.S. Navy trains dolphins to find underwater explosives. Animals do not set off explosives, but boats can. If these **bombs** are not found, they can sink ships and hurt people. The dolphins find them before they explode.

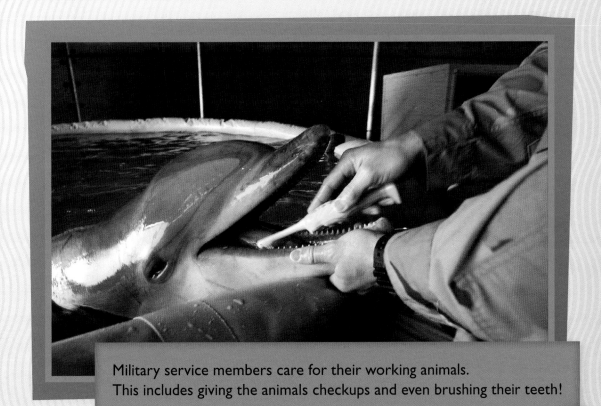

Military service members care for their working animals. This includes giving the animals checkups and even brushing their teeth!

Hoofed Helpers

In the past, horses were one of the most important military animals. Soldiers rode them into battle. They used horses to carry people and supplies. Today, soldiers mostly ride in vehicles. So, horses are used little.

Today, horses are often a part of military parades and ceremonies.

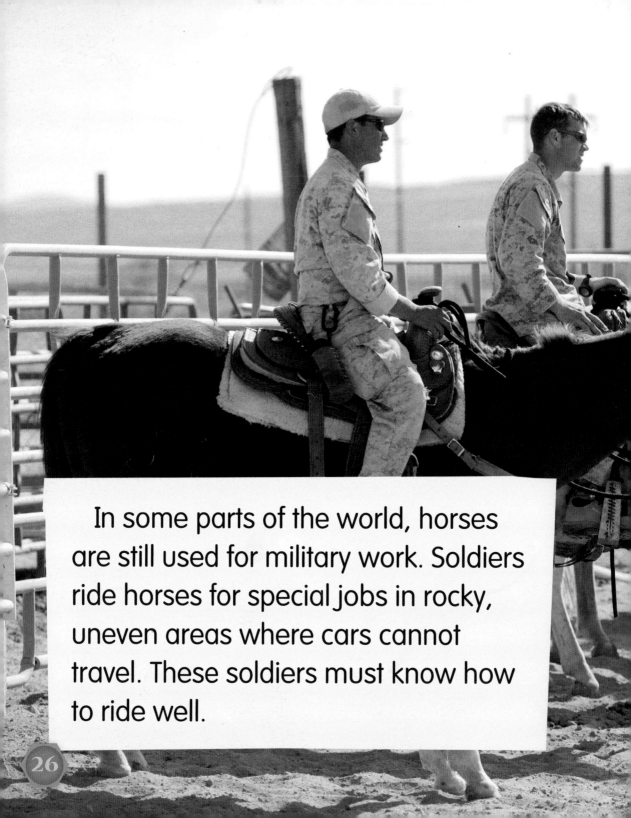

In some parts of the world, horses are still used for military work. Soldiers ride horses for special jobs in rocky, uneven areas where cars cannot travel. These soldiers must know how to ride well.

Some soldiers use horses regularly. Learning to ride and care for the horses is an important part of their training.

Gifted Workers

Military animals use their natural skills to do many important tasks. They work to keep people safe. And, they help protect countries and save lives. This is meaningful work!

Soldiers and animals often form friendships while working together.

The Animal Times

Camels in the Army

In the 1800s, the U.S. Army had a Camel Corps. Some thought that camels would be well suited for the hot deserts in the Southwest. But, the experiment failed. The camels were unpleasant, and they scared mules.

Service Record

Dogs have served the U.S. military since the American Revolution. The first official military dog training was during World War II.

Important Words

bomb (BAHM) a case filled with something that explodes when set off.

clamp to fasten together with a clamp. A clamp is something that tightly holds parts together.

echolocation (eh-koh-loh-KAY-shuhn) a process for locating distant or unseen objects by using sound waves.

enforcement (ihn-FAWR-smuhnt) the action of carrying out something, such as laws.

scout to explore an area to gain a better understanding of something.

tank a large, armed war vehicle that moves on tracks.

Web Sites

To learn more about military animals, visit ABDO Publishing Company online. Web sites about military animals are featured on our Book Links page. These links are routinely monitored and updated to provide the most current information available.

www.abdopublishing.com

Index